Author By ken seng
Twilight Guardians:
Solitary Glow at Dusk

Book Synopsis:

Set within the mystical confines of Nightfall University, where humans and supernatural beings coexist in a patchwork of academia and seclusion, "Twilight Guardians: Solitary Glow at Dusk" unravels a tale imbued with arcane prophecies and the convergence of celestial bodies. As the forgotten covenants and guardians of yore blur into obscurity, a sinuous vortex of both natural and preternatural forces sweeps through this institution, shadowy specters edging in as the stars align.

Eleanor, a mere human girl, and Orion, of enigmatic lineage, find their destinies entwined and compelled to navigate the brewing tempest. With darkness congregating and ancient forces at play, the unlikely duo must rally disparate campus factions to confront looming threats, internal fears, and misconceptions. Through a labyrinth of alliances, crises, and maturation, they halt the cataclysm foretold by legends and peel back layers of secrets buried deep within the annals of Nightfall University.

Their adventure fosters a peace fought on behalf of their realms, revealing a resonance and understanding between them. They usher in a new era of collaboration, guided by ancient tales and enhanced by modern knowledge, where supernatural academics become integral to the curriculum, not shrouded in the mystique of dread.

In "Twilight Guardians: Solitary Glow at Dusk," we witness the inception of an era marked by achievements and beginnings. Eleanor and Orion stand not just as harbingers of change but as symbols of a synergistic future. As they tread together through the tranquil, snow-kissed grounds of Nightfall University, the future of the school and its inhabitants is brightened by their courage and insight.

Table of contents

One could not ignore the grandeur of Nightfall University as the shiny black sedan made its way through the wrought-iron gates.

"This is it, Nightfall U," whisper-murmured Orion Derleth as he looked at the massive grey-brick buildings through the frosty car window. The serene night was even more chilling than usual.

"Alrighty then," said the amiable driver before he carried Orion's luggage to 'The Lupus Dormitory', where the new life of Orion was about to begin.

A tall, lanky guy, James, his roommate, welcomed him. "Got lost in the courtyard labyrinth, did you?" James winked. Together, they navigated the intricacies of dormitory life, trying to make the small, foreign room feel like home.

That very night, as the clock struck 2 AM, an uncanny sensation chilled Orion's spine; the familiar rumble deep within as the full moon shone brightly in the sky. His heart pounded as his body writhed in energy; he made his way out quietly, not wanting to wake James.

Years of experience had taught Orion that running could ease his unsolicited transformation. He sprinted across the vast field, his breathing heavy, his pulse quickened. He found solace in the run, and the exertion provided him control.

As he was catching his breath, his keen ears picked up an approaching murmur. He instinctively hid behind a tall oak tree. A group of students wandered into the moonlit field.

"Eleanor, you sure we are going the right way?" one of them asked.

"I'm sure, Lucas. We should just trust the moon," an unmistakable voice replied. It was Eleanor, the girl whose smile in the freshers' meet had stayed with him.

"Yeah, like it's guiding us or something," another student chimed in as they walked right where Orion was a moment ago. His heart pounded against his chest, resonating with the whispers of his lineage.

No dialogue about the mystical Nightfall U was complete without mentioning the lake; when the full moon shone brightly, the lake would mirror its luminance.

As Orion made his way back, his silver-grey eyes glimmered as he crossed paths with Dr. Monroe, an enigmatic figure of the university. "A fine night, Mr. Derleth," said Dr. Monroe. He adjusted his glasses, his expression unreadable as he continued his stroll. Did he know? Orion wondered.

Lying on his bed, the familiar exhaustion seeped in. He quickly scribbled in his moonphase journal about the night while James snored blissfully. A personal note of intensity, transformations, and how he ran off to the field.

"First night at Nightfall U," he murmured before drifting into sleep, unaware of the adventures looming over his university life.

I'm glad you're interested in continuing the story of Orion at Nightfall University. However, writing 2500 words in a single response exceeds the character and word constraints for this platform. I'd be happy to continue the story in smaller segments that connect to create a larger narrative. Here is a continuation from the previous segment, conforming to the limitations:

Chapter 2: "Whispers in the Woods"

Orion awoke to the rhythm of an autumn rain patting against the window and James's voice filling the room. "I hear the woods here are a maze of wonders. Shall we explore after class?"

He rubbed the sleep from his eyes. "Sure," Orion replied, eager to know the woods that held the secrets of his nocturnal escapades.

The day passed in a blur of heavy syllabi and keen professors, with Dr. Monroe's enigmatic gaze emerging in crowded hallways and echoing chambers of lecture halls.

After the sun dipped below the horizon, painting the sky a crimson hue, added vigor arose in Orion's steps. He sensed the proximity of the woods whispering ancient songs only his ears could perceive.

As they stepped into the verdant embrace of the towering trees, an electric charge filled the air. "Local legend says werewolves roam these woods," James said with a half-mocking laugh as they navigated the winding paths.

Orion' s pulse quickened. "Werewolves, huh?" he played along, his tone laced with forced humor, but his mind raced with ancestral warnings.

Their banter was cut short by a rustle nearby. A doe, caught in the tension of their presence, dashed into the brush.

James's eyes widened. "Did you hear that story about the Lupus spirit protecting this forest?" Orion fought to keep his expression neutral.

Amid their trek, they stumbled upon a clearing where the remnants of a bonfire spoke of gatherings most secret. "What do you reckon happens here?" James pondered.

"Probably just an ordinary campus bonfire party," Orion suggested, pushing down the memory of tribal ceremonies from his lineage.

Unease settled in as the night crept upon them, and Orion felt the call of the unseen moon. He excused himself, citing a sudden headache. The truth, as always, was more compelling.

He found solace under the canopy of the ancient woods, the pressures of his dual existence weighing on him. He knew he couldn't outrun his truth forever. The whispers of the woods seemed to agree.

Back in his dormitory, Orion found himself lost in thought. "Why me?" he muttered under his breath. The whispering woods offered no reply.

The full moon was still a few nights away, but the tension was building. His instincts were becoming more potent. As he gazed at the moon from his dormitory window, his keen eyes could almost make out the silhouette of the ancient wolf spirit from his family's tales. But was it real, or was it just his overwrought imagination?

Orion's thoughts were interrupted by James, who returned grinning ear to ear. "Guess who scored an invite to the legendary bonfire party?" James brandished a slip of paper, an invite etched onto it with symbols so ancient, only Orion knew what they implied.

"Great, that should be fun," Orion said, forcing a smile. At the back of his mind, he couldn't help but wonder if the bonfire party was connected to the mysteries of the woods.

A few days later, on the night of the party, students flocked to the clearing in the woods where Orion and James had previously stumbled upon the remnants of a bonfire. Orion noted Dr. Monroe among the crowd. As the bonfire was set ablaze, a chorus of howls echoed from deep within the woods. The energy in the crowd was palpable. The unlimited supply of marshmallows, soda, and folklore tales circulating throughout the crowd made it a quintessential bonfire night, yet Orion felt an underlying current of something more.

As the fire crackled under the moonlight, stories of werewolves, shape-shifters, and mythical moon spirits filled the air. Unbeknownst to the others, Orion felt an unusual connection with these tales, his mind pieces together voices from the past.

Suddenly, Eleanor, the girl he' d remembered from the moonlit field, was by his side. "Legend has it that the bonfire keeps the werewolves away. But I ask you, what if someone among us is a werewolf?" She looked at him, her eyes glistening in the firelight, the half-joked question hanging ominously in the air.

Could she have sensed his secret? Orion wondered. But before he could react, Eleanor was pulled away, leaving Orion with a lingering sense of unease and unanswered questions.

His mind echoed with the whispers of the woods as he departed from the party early, the pull of the moon more potent than before. The bonfire's tales added layers to his worries, his secret simultaneously a blessing and a curse. His heart pounded in his chest as he escaped to the serenity of the moonlit field again. The whispers had grown louder, the call of the moon stronger, and Orion knew he wouldn't be able to hide his secret for much longer.

Life at Nightfall University unfolded in the overlap of the ordinary and the mystical, and the following days were filled with classes, assignments, and the impending burden of Orion's secret. His trips to the moonlit field became more frequent and coupled with the whispers of the woods.

It wasn't until he had another chance encounter with Eleanor in the university library that his worries took a surprising turn.

"I'm studying the folklore of this place," Eleanor explained, her table spread with ancient texts and illustrations of mythical moon spirits. "It's for our cultural tradition assignment," she added.

Orion swallowed, the echo of her question from the bonfire night circling in his head. "We have legends of werewolves in our family too," he shared, risking a glance at her.

Eleanor's eyes lit up with curiosity. "Really? And don't you think our university, with its legends and lunar ties, is perfect for understanding such mysteries?"

Orion nodded tentatively, surprised by her open-mindedness and intrigued by her interest in the university's cultural history.

One late evening during their research, Eleanor brought up the university lake, known as the "Moon's Mirror," famous for its luminosity during the full moon. Legends suggested the lake held mystical powers amplified by the moon.

The notion of the "Moon's Mirror" and the upcoming full moon gave Orion an idea. Perhaps he could harness the lake's energy to control his transformations.

On the peak of the approaching full moon, Orion decided to visit the lake. As moonlight danced off the rippling water's surface, a feeling of calm washed over him.

He barely noticed the crunching leaves behind him until Eleanor's voice broke his reverie. "The moon really does mirror in the lake," she marveled.

Startled, Orion tucked away his family medallion that he was clutching in his hand. "Couldn't sleep, Eleanor?" A nervous laugh escaped his lips as he tried to gauge her reaction.

"No," she shrugged, her eyes fixed on the moon's reflection on the glass-like water, missing the medallion. "There's a lot about Nightfall University that keeps me up."

Unbeknownst to her, her words echoed Orion's predicament. The secrets of this university and his lineage were intertwined, and as the moon mirrored perfectly onto the lake, he wondered whether they would mirror onto his university life too.

Though they stood together under the same moonlight, each was lost in their thoughts, connected yet separate. There was a kindred spirit between them, one that could either deepen the mystery or unearth the truth.

The serene night wore on, and the gentle lapping of lake waters against the shore created a tranquil soundtrack. Orion, usually restless before the full moon, found himself unusually at peace beside Eleanor.

"Wouldn' t it be something," Eleanor said softly, breaking the silence between them, "if those legends were true? If the people connected to them walked among us?"

Eleanor's innocent musings struck a chord within Orion. "Maybe they do," he said. "Maybe they' re just waiting for the right time to show themselves." His voice was even, but inside, his heart raced at his boldness - a coy dance around the truth he harbored.

She turned to face him, the moonlight casting her in silver tones. "I think some things are meant to be kept secret. Like a sacred pact with the night," Eleanor mused, a mysterious smile on her lips.

Orion nodded, feeling the gravity of her words as they echoed his own inner conflicts. Yet her presence was comforting, a surprising anchor in the complex tides he was navigating.

They decided to sit in silence, absorbing the night's magic. Orion couldn' t help but let his gaze drift to Eleanor, wondering to what extent she understood the night's secrets.

As the night deepened, the time for parting arrived. "Thanks for... this," Orion gestured towards the lake, "it's been... enlightening."

Eleanor smiled, "Anytime, Orion. Goodnight."

As she walked away, Orion felt the pull of the moon, stronger and more demanding. The magic of the night couldn't stave off the inevitable forever. It was time for him to retreat into the woods, to surrender to the part of him that was more than human.

As he reached the familiar seclusion among the trees, Orion began his transformation. His body resounded with ancestral power. And yet, tonight was different—the calmness from the lake lingered, his thoughts a clear stream rather than a turbulent torrent. For the first time, he could remember every moment of his transformation. The night was full of revelations, and as his senses heightened, a newfound control anchored his spirit.

The dawn found him sitting at the edge of the forest, eyes reflecting the depth of his experiences. He was more than the legends foretold, more than what he had seen in the mirror of the lake. He was the sum of all these parts—man and beast, myth and reality.

Orion made his way back to the dormitory, wondering what the next night would bring, and how Eleanor fitted into the tapestry of his story.

Orion's university life bore the mark of a dual existence. In this chapter of his story, he battled with the challenges of mundane academic pursuits and the expectations of his ancient lineage. With each passing day, he became more attuned to the whispers of the woods and more adept at handling his transformation. The Moon's Mirror was undoubtedly a significant factor in this newfound balance.

He found an unconventional ally in Eleanor. Their shared fascination with the university's lunar legends became the catalyst for a deep friendship. Eleanor was oblivious to how close these legends were to Orion' s truth—but how long could he keep his secret hidden from her?

In their folklore study group, Eleanor enthusiastically discussed her findings about ancient lunar rituals, the folklore surrounding them, and the impact on those with lunar lineage.

Eleanor's interest in the subject astonished Orion. "Your dedication to these legends is impressive, Eleanor. It's like they're near to your heart," he said, gauging her reaction.

Eleanor shrugged. "Perhaps. Or perhaps it's just the allure of the unknown," she responded, her focus back on intricate illustrations of the Moon's Mirror and elaborate lunar symbology in an old book.

One night, Orion and Eleanor led their study group on a night trek through the Nightfall woods for an assignment. Navigating through whispering trees under the celestial canopy, they reached the Moon's Mirror.

While the others busied themselves with field notes, Orion and Eleanor stood by the lake, the shimmering surface mirroring the star-studded sky. Orion felt a surge of supernatural energy; his lunar senses were heightened near the full moon.

Suddenly, they heard a distant howl echoing through the forest, sending a hush across the group. The howl was haunting, but Orion recognized it—it was his call to the moon from one of his transformations.

Eleanor glanced at Orion, a knowing look in her eyes. In that silence, their connection deepened, marked by shared mysteries and hundreds of unsaid words.

Two paths lay before Orion—hide his truth or embrace the mighty lineage he belonged to. His decision didn't merely affect him but now Eleanor and their college lives. The echoes of the howls served as a reminder of his destiny—that he was an integral part of the lunar legends engulfing Nightfall University.

As the howl faded into the abyss, the group trembled with a combined fear and fascination. Yet, amidst the choir of whispers and gasps, Eleanor remained calm. Her eyes met Orion's for a brief second—sparkling with an unsaid understanding.

The night passed, and despite the unsettling howl, the group's interest in Nightfall's legends only intensified. Orion, on the other hand, found his thoughts circling around Eleanor. Her calmness, her acceptance of the eccentricities, everything about her was a solace in an otherwise convoluted existence.

Days turned into weeks, and the cycle of learning and transformation continued. The shifts that were once agonizing now felt natural, as if he was merely stepping into another aspect of himself.

Orion's bond with Eleanor deepened. They spent countless hours beside the Moon's Mirror, lost in legend-laced discussions, the secrecy of the moon their only witness. Eleanor's passion for the lunar lore never dulled, but Orion started noticing the peculiar way she'd enunciate certain aspects of the legends, as if she were hinting at something.

One day, Eleanor brought up the werewolf legend. "Do you ever wonder, Orion?" she asked, her voice low, almost a whisper. "What if these legends aren't just tales from the past? What if some are living these legends right now, shadowed and silent?"

Orion sat immobilized, his heart pounded loudly in the silence following her words. She was closer to the truth than ever, too close. He needed to tread carefully.

Before he could respond, Eleanor reached for something in her bag. She extended her hand toward him, revealing an ancestral locket. It bore strong similarities to Orion's family medallion.

"I found it in my grandmother's belongings," she said, her gaze locked on the locket. "She told me tales of our lineage tracing back to the guardianship of the Moon's Mirror. I didn't realize the depth of those words until I saw this."

Orion sat in stunned silence. A torrent of realization washed over him as he absorbed Eleanor's words. The subtle hints, the fascinated interest in folklore—it was all making sense. Eleanor was as much a part of the lunar mystery as he was.

A significant revelation brought Orion to the crossroads of his secrets—acceptance of dual lives, the inexplicable bond with Eleanor, and the truth that Nightfall University was much more than an academic haven. It was where the threads of their destinies intertwined, under the ageless gaze of the lunar cycle.

Chapter 5: "Revelation in the Shadows"

School life swirled around Orion with the usual frenzy of assignments, looming deadlines, and the drama of campus politics, yet he now moved through it all with a new perspective. Eleanor' s revelation had sent ripples through his world, and those ripples had not yet stilled.

Their conversations became hushed exchanges filled with the gravity of their lineages. They were descendants of the night, bound by the ancient traditions and modern secrets.

While Eleanor's ancestors had been guardians, Orion' s had been the very subject of those legends — a fact that remained his to share. His trust for Eleanor grew with each interaction, yet there was a fear of the untamed consequences sharing his truth could unleash.

Meanwhile, the Moon' s Mirror seemed to beckon them, a silent whisper calling to the core of their beings. They both had pieces of a puzzle that the other needed. What was once just a place of quiet contemplation became a clandestine meeting point where the seams of the supernatural world met the fabric of the mortal realm.

One night, as the full moon cast its argent spell over the Earth, they met again by the lake. The air was charged with an unspoken anticipation. The time for masquerade was coming to an end.

Eleanor faced Orion, her eyes reflecting a serious determination. "Orion, we cannot dance around the truth any longer. This place, our heritage... it's calling to us. Don't you feel it?"

Her words hung heavy in the air, and Orion took a deep breath. The powerful lunar energy filled his lungs, fortifying his resolve.

"Yes," he said, the word resonating with the weight of his admissions. "I feel it, Eleanor. My connection with this place runs deeper than you may realize."

Eleanor' s eyes widened, a silent encouragement for him to continue.

Orion looked up at the moon, and then back at Eleanor. "The legends we discussed, they speak of guardians and the beings they protect—who are bound to the moon, who change with its phases."

Her breath hitched as understanding dawned. "The werewolves..."

"Yes," Orion admitted, his voice barely above a whisper, "I am a descendant of those very creatures. I am the living embodiment of the legends we have studied."

The revelation hit Eleanor like a wave, yet she stood unwavering. Instead of fear, Orion saw intrigue mixed with a kind of kinship in her eyes.

"I suspected," she confessed. "The signs were there, but knowing the legends and seeing their truth are two entirely different things."

The night seemed to hold its breath, waiting for their next move. There, beside the lake that had seen reflections of countless generations, they began to weave the new chapter of an age-old saga.

With the revelation out in the open, Orion felt a new freedom—a liberation from his solitary confinement to his secret.

The days that followed were a whirlwind. Orion and Eleanor spent more time together, their conversations now layered with a mutual acceptance of their shared heritage. Amidst the ordinary humdrum of student life, they explored their supernatural destinies with a buzzing excitement interwoven with a somber understanding of their responsibilities.

Orion noticed Eleanor's intense eagerness to understand his transformations. After all, it wasn't just about legends anymore. It was sure reality, as real as the moon that hung in the night sky, as vital as the blood that coursed through their veins.

During the day, they were just ordinary students attending lectures, submitting assignments. But, when nightfall arrived, they tread into the territory of legends and secrets, their destinies intertwined under the watchful eyes of the Moon's Mirror.

Within this extraordinary balance, they found a strange solace. Eleanor delighted in every revelation about her guardian heritage, and Orion basked in the growing comfort that he was no longer alone.

One full moon night, Eleanor voiced a question that had been lingering in her mind. "Orion," she started, her voice urgent yet soft, "Can I see it? Your transformation, how it all happens?"

Orion paused. The transformations were deeply personal, intense moments for him, but the earnest plea in Eleanor's eyes stirred a sense of trust. Perhaps, it would be different with her. Perhaps, it could bring them closer.

He measured his heartbeat against the rhythmic lapping of the lake waves for a few moments before responding. "Alright, Eleanor. We shall face this tide together."

On the next full moon, under the lunar goddess's empathetic gaze, Eleanor witnessed Orion's transformation. Fear was overshadowed by awe as Orion morphed into his ethereal wolf form under the silvery moonlight - a creature of elegance and power, gentle and yet with a raw ferocity.

As he allowed her into this world, Eleanor watched with a mixture of reverence and wonder, her guardian instincts taking over. Not once did she flinch. Instead, she moved closer, reaching out to touch the silken fur. Their eyes locked, a moment that captured centuries of folkloric harmony in a shared glance.

Their exploration evolved beyond whispers by the lake and ancient legends. It emboldened them to face the underlying truths, to understand the past, and to create a way for their intertwined future. Uncharted territories waited to be traversed, and shadows of enigma yearned to be illuminated.

From the cocoon of secrecy to the revelation in the shadows, Orion and Eleanor were deconstructing their lore and rebuilding it in their own image - in acceptance, in courage, and in unity.

Chapter 6: "The Gathering Storm"

As autumn crept upon Nightfall University, the season mirrored the transformation in Orion and Eleanor's journey. The air was crisply laden with whispers of change, and the world around them bore a vivid palette of auras as if acknowledging the shift within their souls.

In this period of metamorphosis, the knowledge they shared between them grew ever more profound, no longer confined to personal revelation but expanding towards the promise of action. Eleanor, with her newly discovered guardian ancestry, and Orion, embracing his hereditary power, began to sense a stirring beyond the confines of their understanding—a storm gathering at the edges of their awareness.

The Moon's Mirror, once a serene rendezvous, now played host to discussions of urgency. Strange occurrences, earlier dismissed as mere folklore, started to manifest with unnerving frequency around Nightfall. Whispers among the students spoke of shadows moving of their own accord, and inexplicable chills that whispered of ancient unrest.

"It seems the veil between our world and the old legends is thinning," Eleanor observed one evening as they sat by the lake, watching the reflection of the twilight sky.

Orion nodded, his gaze distant. "And I fear what we've learned, what we've become, is entwined with whatever is to come."

Their academic pursuits took a parallel track with their exploration of the supernatural, intertwining their studies with the understanding of the ancient energies that pulsed beneath the surface of Nightfall. It wasn't long before they discovered references to a convergence—a rare alignment of celestial bodies that could either restore balance or cause chaos in the fabric between the worlds.

With the convergence predicted to occur before the end of the semester, Orion and Eleanor knew they had little time to prepare. They delved deeper, seeking knowledge from forbidden texts hidden in the library's restricted section and consulting professors who were rumored to be more than mere academics.

The urgency of their mission drew them closer. Their bond, now forged in mutual purpose and shared secrets, became their beacon. Together, they pieced together the puzzle, uncovering the need for a guardian and a being of the night to stand together at the convergence—to face whatever might emerge from the shadows.

As the signs around them grew more ominous, and the whispers among the student body turned to anxiety and fear, Orion and Eleanor prepared. They trained in secret, Orion mastering the control over his transformations, and Eleanor honing her latent abilities, linked to the energies of the earth and moon.

Their nights were consumed with preparations, each understanding the role they were to play in the coming confrontation. It was a dance of destiny they engaged in, with the entirety of Nightfall University, unbeknownst to most of its inhabitants, serving as the stage.

As the day of the convergence approached, the air around Nightfall thickened with anticipation. Orion and Eleanor stood together, more united than ever, ready to face the gathering storm. They were the legacy of legends, the bridge between worlds, and the hope of harmony. Whatever lay ahead, they knew their strength lay not just in their shared heritage or newfound powers, but in something far more potent—each other.

The convergence was not just a challenge; it was a test of their strength and the validation of their heritage. Orion and Eleanor, creating a synergy of their abilities, were Nightfall's only hope against whatever might cast its dark shadow with the upcoming celestial alignment.

Orion's nights were filled with strenuous physical training, mastering his strength, speed, and predatory instincts, while his days were consumed with study. He explored the unique bond his lineage shared with the lunar cycles and experimented with his ability to transform outside the full moon's influence, discovering a newfound control over his transformative powers.

Eleanor, for her part, discovered she could tap into the Earth's natural forces, channeling them into a formidable shield or a potent attack when necessary. With each sunset, Eleanor became more adept at invoking these guardian abilities. Her spirit danced in harmony with the elements, summoning the wind to her bidding or harnessing the rich energy of the soil beneath her feet.

Time seemed to hurtle towards the day of the convergence. The days grew shorter, the nights longer, the air heavier, as if nature itself sensed the impending event. A palpable tension hung over Nightfall.

Finally, the day of the convergence arrived. An unusual calm had settled over Nightfall University. Students walked around campus, whispers of worry circulating among them, their concerns dismissed as superstition by the unaware.

As nightfall descended, Orion and Eleanor stood by the Moon's Mirror, their hearts echoing the same calm before the storm. The sky overhead was a theater of stars and constellations, with the moon at the zenith, charging the air with a powerful energy. It was time.

The moment happened without pomp and circumstance. One minute the world was as they knew it, and the next, it had changed. A ripple in reality began at the Moon's Mirror, growing until it birthed a shadowy figure radiating a chilling darkness that made the whispers of dread among the students feel like lullabies.

Orion and Eleanor, with their combined might, readied themselves. Orion, now a fearsome wolf under the moon's glow, roared a challenge while Eleanor, a fierce and formidable guardian, stood grounded, her body a conduit of elemental energy, her intentions steely.

Otherworldly wails filled the air as they pressed forward. The two symbols of an ancient pact, a

guardian and a being of the night, shouldered the
fate of their world. The battle, as violent and
fearsome as those of the cryptic tales, began
under the watchful eyes of the stars.

Chapter 7: "Dawn of A New Era"

With the conclusion of the celestial convergence,
the aftermath left both Orion and Eleanor
breathless. The energy that radiated from the
Moon's Mirror, once a source of ominous
foreboding, now felt cleansed, as if the very air
around them hummed with a new life. The
shadow that had dared to disrupt the harmony of
their world had been vanquished, not just by their
powers but by the unity and understanding they
had forged between their worlds.

As the first light of dawn crept over the horizon,
casting golden hues over the lake, a profound
sense of peace settled over Nightfall University.
The students, who had spent the night restless

with anxiety, now emerged from their dormitories, drawn to the tranquility that seemed to envelop the campus.

Orion, now in his human form, stood side by side with Eleanor, watching the new day unfold. They were exhausted, physically and emotionally, but the dawn brought with it a sense of accomplishment and hope.

"We did it," Eleanor whispered, her voice filled with wonder. "We really did it."

Orion nodded, a small smile gracing his lips. "Together," he affirmed, gazing into the horizon, where the night's darkness had given way to the day' s light.

Their victory was not without its lessons. In the aftermath of the battle, as they helped to mend what had been disrupted on campus, Orion and Eleanor understood that their fight was not against the shadows but against the fear and misunderstanding that often bred in ignorance. They had united not just their powers but their communities, bridging a gap that had long stood between the natural and the supernatural.

The days that followed saw a transformation not just in Orion and Eleanor but within Nightfall University itself. With the truth of the convergence and its handling now open, discussions began—led by Orion and Eleanor—on integrating knowledge of the supernatural with the university's curriculum. A new era of understanding and coexistence dawned, one where myths and legends were no longer just stories but a part of their daily lives, to be respected and learned from.

Eleanor took the initiative to establish a council, comprising beings of both worlds, to oversee the peace and share knowledge between the supernatural and human communities. Orion, with his unique heritage, served as a bridge, a symbol of the unity that could be achieved.

As autumn turned to winter, Orion and Eleanor found themselves often reflecting on the events that had unfolded. What had started as a search for identity and belonging had evolved into a journey that transcended their personal stories, affecting the lives around them and shaping the future of Nightfall University.

Their journeys had taught them about strength, not just the kind that could fend off shadows, but the strength found in trust, in unity, and in the acceptance of differences. They had learned that true power lay in the ability to embrace one's heritage and use it for the greater good, to illuminate the darkness not with force, but with understanding and light.

As they stood together, watching the snowflakes gently fall onto the tranquil grounds of the university, there was a serene confidence about them. They were the Guardians of Nightfall, the preservers of peace, and the harbingers of a new era where shadows and light danced together, creating a harmony that was stronger for its diversity.

The legacy of Orion and Eleanor, of their battle and unity, would be a beacon for future generations, a testament to the fact that even in the darkest of times, there can emerge a light strong enough to forge a new path—a Dawn of a New Era.

The remainder of the academic year passed in a harmonious flurry. Nightfall University flourished in this new environment, its students and faculty finding a unique resonance with this preserved peace. Orion and Eleanor became not just the faces of this change but active participants, guiding the university into an era where acceptance and knowledge became the norm.

Eleanor worked closely with the faculty, introducing courses that intertwined their existing curriculum with an expanded understanding of the supernatural world. History classes now spoke of the true founding of Nightfall and the pact between the guardians and beings of the night. Biology and environmental studies began exploring the influence of lunar cycles on the fauna and flora around them, lending an enhanced appreciation for the Earth's natural rhythms.

Orion, through his council sessions, made strides in integrating supernatural beings into the university's social fabric. Activities were organized where werewolves offered lessons in survival skills during camping trips or night walks, and elemental guardians held sessions on understanding nature's signals. The barrier between 'them' and 'us' began to blur, replaced by a collective 'we'.

This newfound unity was not without its hurdles. Eleanor faced opposition from professors stuck in their conventional ways, some refusing to change, others dismissing their efforts as fanciful. But with every challenge, Eleanor remained undeterred. She knew that the path towards understanding had always been paved with resistance.

Orion, too, faced his share of trials. Not all of the supernatural beings were keen on revealing their existence to humans, viewing it as a risk to their long-preserved secrecy. Yet, Orion reminded them that hiding did not equate to peace. He assured them that this wasn't about exposure, but about creating a safer environment for all—the supernatural beings included.

As they navigated these challenges, Orion and Eleanor found solace and friendship in each other. They had begun this journey as strangers, separated by their differing experiences, yet destiny had intertwined their paths. Now, they stood together as partners, their strength and resolve fanned by the collective trust they had braved against the storm they had faced together.

Perhaps the most significant testament to this new era was the change in the atmosphere around Nightfall. Where once rumors and whispers of the supernatural caused fear and distrust, they were now met with curiosity, followed by understanding. The students, once divided, were now united under the shared banner of knowledge and coexistence.

As the ultimate symbol of their success, at the end of the academic year, a grand festival was held: "The Harmony Festival". This event celebrated the unity and the peace between the human and supernatural worlds, becoming a tradition that would be carried forward to mark the dawn of a new era in Nightfall University.

And so, under the moonlit sky and against the backdrop of laughter and cheer, Orion and Eleanor stood together, their hearts swelling with satisfaction and hope. They had ignited a change that would illuminate many generations to come, a beacon of peace and acceptance in a world once towering with division. Their legacy was just beginning...

The end